XAVIER

THANKU

contents

THANKU

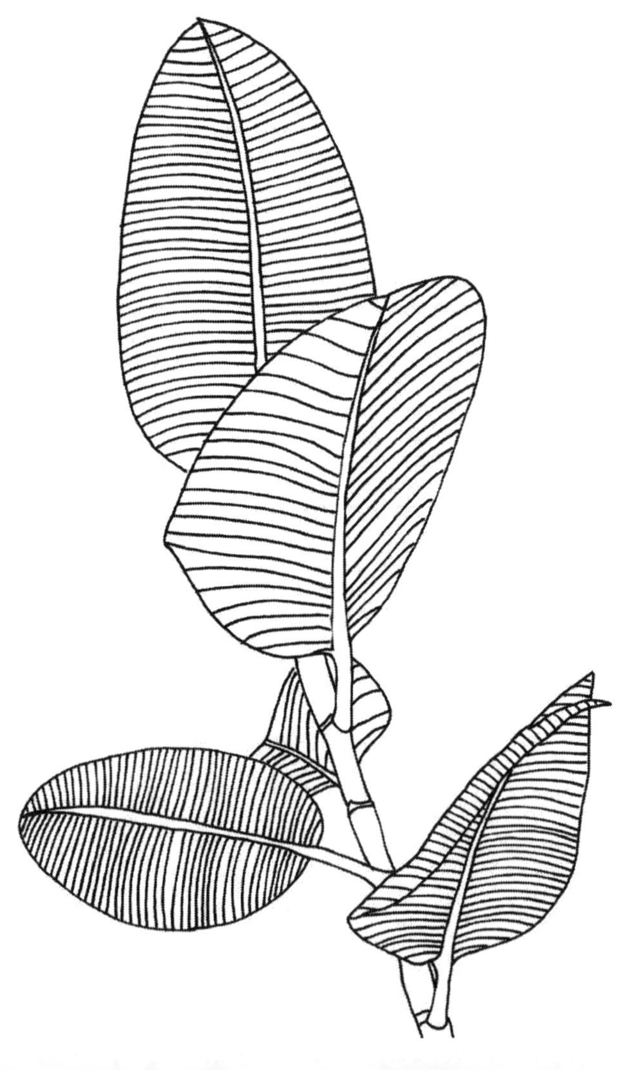

SELF

forgive me
for what has not been done
for i've
only taken the time to perfect
what not
so many have set out to do
not to be found as a perfectionist
i shall never attempt to dishonor
the higher existence
for when i write
i write with intentions
i write and then reflect
as if
the words were already written
and when these words are visible
to the naked eye
they will find their soul

the messenger

through God these words are written
to connect
guide
and
give love
in a time
when love can be
forgotten

let us remember

feel these words from miles away
even though i'm not physically there
my words can and will
touch your soul
in many ways

THANKU

i'm constantly creating a world of love, beauty, and peace
there will be people who will want to destroy my world
some will want to live, grow and die in my world
no matter who comes into my world
i will always have the ability to change, improve or get rid
of things in my world
some say what if this world we all live in
was full of love, beauty, and peace
over time, this world would be a better place
i say, what if everyone created their own world
of love, beauty, and peace
this world would change in a heartbeat

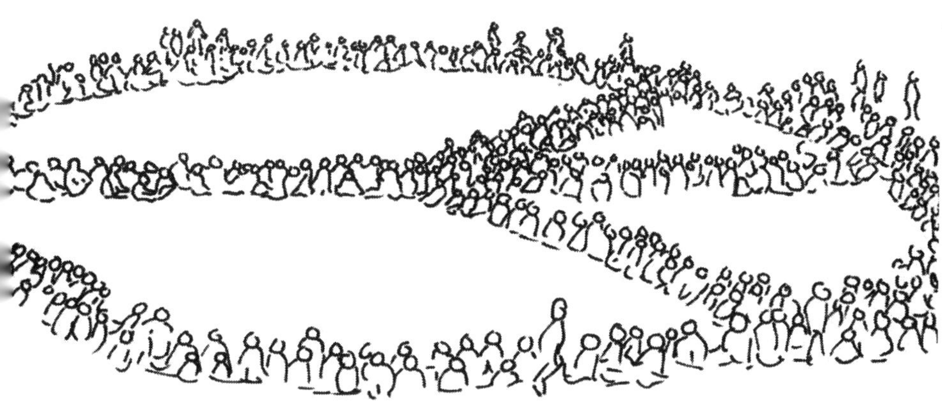

you cannot cope with the people
if you're not among the people
you can not hear their cries
when you speak too loud
you cannot feel their pain
when you have no touch
they needed this moment
and you took it from them
as if it belonged to you
not one piece was left the same
not one soul was taken into consideration
and no one was able to stop it
for you may not realize it now
but eventually
all things come to an end
and all pain
looks for revenge

your mind has been
distracting you
from
what your heart
already knows

most look on the outside to find
what is already on the inside
it's not until they are alone
and in silence
They realize

meditation

deciding
to be
in complete solitude
is the first step
in spending quality time
with yourself

separating yourself from others
doesn't need to be justified
we all need time to reflect
and decide
if we are
living a life
that is purposeful

in a world that has shown its flaws
its imperfections
how could i expect to live in
perfection

CAPRICORN
SAGITTARIUS
SCORPIO
LIBRA
VIRGO
LEO
CANCER
GEMINI
TAURUS
ARIES
PISCES
AQUARIUS

a mind that is open
that has no judgment
no distractions
is
as
deep
as
the
s e a

you took me in when i was so naive
you gave my skin thickness
you made me so cold
you made me clever and less gullible
i knew we'd eventually get along
but this love and hate relationship
will eventually grow old

new york city

call me selfish
but i cannot do for others
until i can do for myself

i am willing to struggle
on myself
until i no longer
have baggage
regrets
or insecurities

i was my biggest enemy
until i realized
there was no such thing
as perfection

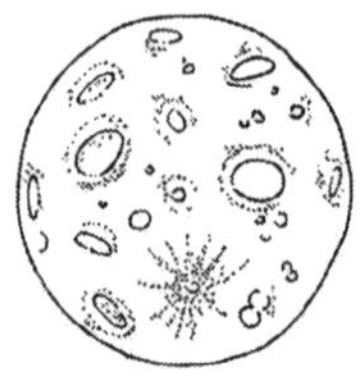

the date last night was one-sided
but i never felt as comfortable as i did
there was no judgment or miscommunication
the love was intense
and i just knew we'd be together forever

date with myself

I have come to a point in life
where nothing feels better
than
self-love
even the love
from another

when we are alone
we tend to feel lonely
like there is no one to talk to
like there is no one to love
when in reality
we have ourselves
we have our thoughts
we have inner voice
we have
ourselves

you will have to
find yourself first
before you can find true love
how can you love another
when you can’t love yourself
loving yourself is
knowing your part
loving yourself is
knowing your worth
loving yourself is
knowing your heart

lost
until i
find
myself

sometimes we need
to go into retrograde
to find our true self

there are many reasons why things are
not working to your advantage
mainly due to insecurities

love yourself

c l u t t e r . . .
not every person in your life
is worth keeping

tears are the only mechanism
that will release all the pain
trapped behind your walls
let them run wild
let them run free
You will feel better afterwards

similar to the rain clouds that pass
your tears won't last forever

have you ever seen a flower grow under water?
i haven't but i know somehow
somewhere
there is one blossoming
in the deepest
and darkest place

if i can't heal myself
i don't know know who can

focus on the now
not tomorrow
not yesterday
be present in the now
be focus on the present
be here in the now

i decided to have no attachments
the universe is meant to flow freely
when there is something
that no longer brings value
or balance to my life
i give it away
and create room for new things

the hardest mission in life
isn't finding a great job
career
college degree
or finding a lover
the hardest thing is
finding yourself
too many people turn old
and miserable
because they never found themselves
but found love
a career
and obtained multiple degrees

never keep
people around who can
find flaws
in your happiness
and joy
in your sadness

find yourself
and you will find your confidence
the things that make you most complete
are the things that one should surrender to
the possibilities are endless
the emotional constraints don't exist
we find it easy to give into things and people
that make us feel whole
but we cannot give entirely into anything
if we don't know ourselves
know our potential

if you don't think
you are one of a kind
start looking at
the type of people you
keep around
and the type of life
you're living

the best version of yourself
depends on those you keep around
either they're going to
build you up
or
bring you down

in the past i used to let people's words
affect my thoughts, feelings and choices
when in reality
they were unhappy with themselves
and needed someone to put down
to lift themselves up

deeper understanding

it's pretty mind opening
to think you know something
then realize
it's something completely different

admit your wrongs
learn from mistakes
keep it moving

majority of the time
when you ask the right questions
it makes all the difference

honesty at times can be a little unsettling
but if we hold back the truth then
we are only encouraging falsification
and disloyalty to ourselves
and others

you can't
expect others
to take
your advice
when you r a r e l y
t a k e
y o u r
o w n

trying to control others
will
forever be
a never-ending
battle

you were a soft flame
that would burn for hours
while
swaying lightly
side to side
dripping slow
creating puddles
that would later turn dry
once you were
burned out

people come and go
they pass like days
months
or seasons

lesson learned or lesson taught?

the moment you begin
listening to yourself
is the moment it will
all start coming together
your heart comes first
mind comes second

you will never come last

starting over
was something i
needed to do
because my soul
needed a
second chance

when you first meet someone
don't give them your whole story
be mysterious
be engaging
give them the cover page
and a little bit of the synopsis

no matter how hard they try
they could never take your happiness
when you manufacture your own

you can't always expect to have happiness
you will have your
ups
downs
and everything else
that falls
in between

reflect
re-evaluate
and give yourself another chance
you deserve it

the zone you have always called comfort
is actually a shield against your true potential
step outside of it
and never look back

the blind will
lead you into blindness
know your direction
at all times
or
find yourself
following the blind
into the dark

eagles fly alone
at high altitudes
and not with
other small birds

egotistical
ideology

when a lot of shit is
going through your head
just let it keep going

guidance exists in a silenced mind

sometimes words are
better left unsaid
if they are
too small
or
too empty

there comes a time of realization
that no other person's opinion matters
only your own

no matter how hard you look
you will never find anyone else
who will push as hard for yourself
than yourself
last thing you want to do is
put all your weight
on the scale of someone else's
And hope
they will remain balanced

LOVE

you take his wrongs
even though
you know
you're right

not worth another fight

i told her many times
she needed to focus more on what she wanted
but she continued to put him first
she searched for happiness through him
and couldn't find her own

being with me
should never be forced
or
taken for granted

sometimes
they have to experience losing you
to realize
they no longer have your heart

you can't expect him to love you
when he doesn't love himself

love will always make you do things
you'd never wanted to do before

wild love is short lived
but true love last forever

losing sleep
wondering if
i'm losing you

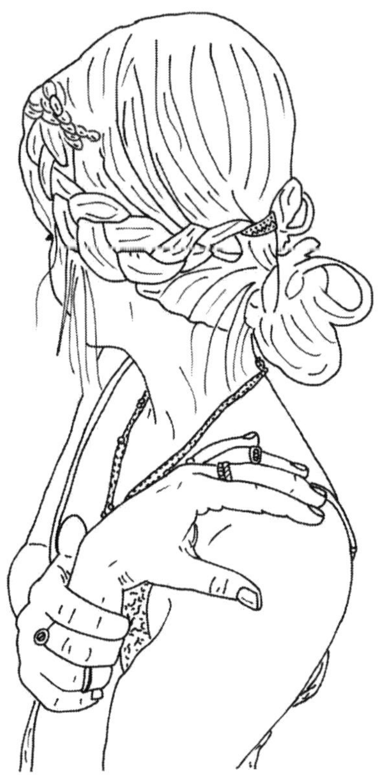

she always looked for acceptance
in other people
which always made her
feel lost

too many times
our conversations got lost
in translation
over text

call me next time

i felt your feelings change
towards me
the moment you began
to look at me
differently

if you feel obligated
to pleasure
or please someone
to feel valued
then you don't know
your
own
worth

if you’re not worth his time
don’t spend yours

anyone that is willing to walk out of your life
has already made the decision to put on their shoes
and walk out the door
with no intentions of coming back

her past still haunts her
she made her walls thick like brick
she developed a taste for hurt
now it's hard to forgive
i told her everything will be okay
her walls began to crumble
in my arms i held her
through her pain and struggle

guarding your heart
is keeping love
at war

surrender...

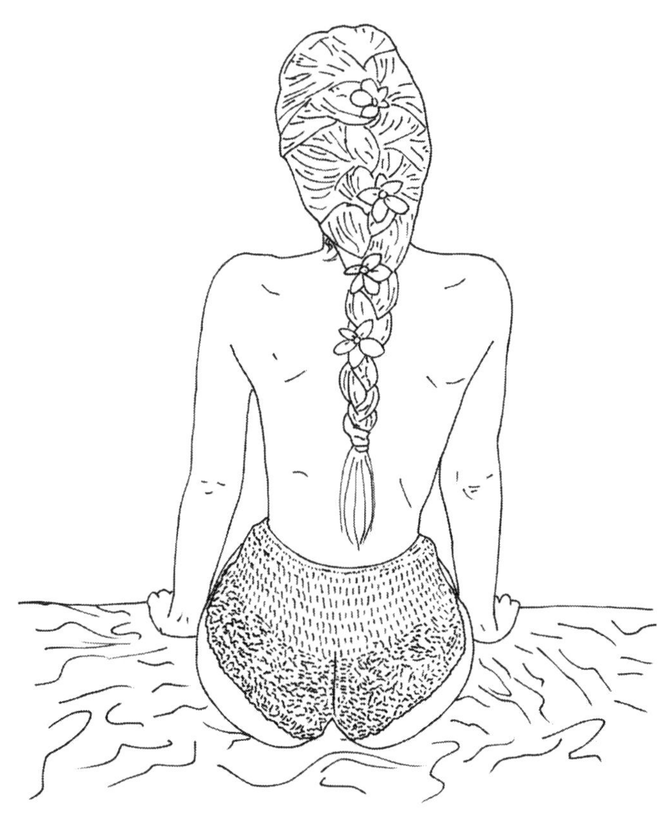

deep in my emotions...
just give me space
just give me time

emotions are expressions in
m
o
t
i
o
n

i love a great conversation
that is well connected

where we both can be transparent
with no judgment
and no miscommunication

taking the words
right out of each other's mouth

you finish my sentence
and I'll finish yours

never take
relationship advice
from friends
who are
single

how could i look you in the eyes
to only tell you a lie
and expect for you to accept it

then i apologize
when the truth comes forth
and expect for you to forget it

you'll never trust me again

appreciate her
or
someone will come along
and show you her worth
for free

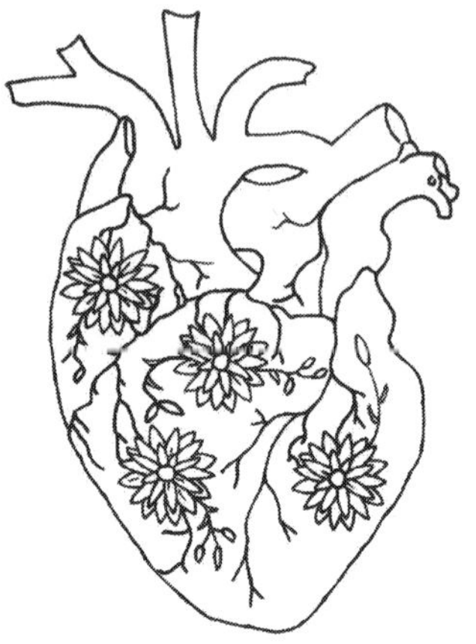

“what if we stop playing these games
and start competing heart to heart?”

til' death do us part
or lies and betrayal

people will never know
what's best for you
so stop people pleasing
and
be yourself

"if i told you that you could do better,
Would you believe me?"

these moments are nothing
without you
i need you
i want you
i breathe for you
teach me how to
l o v e a g a i n

some people love to see us in love
some people hate to see us in love
either way
their feelings could never change
the way we feel about us

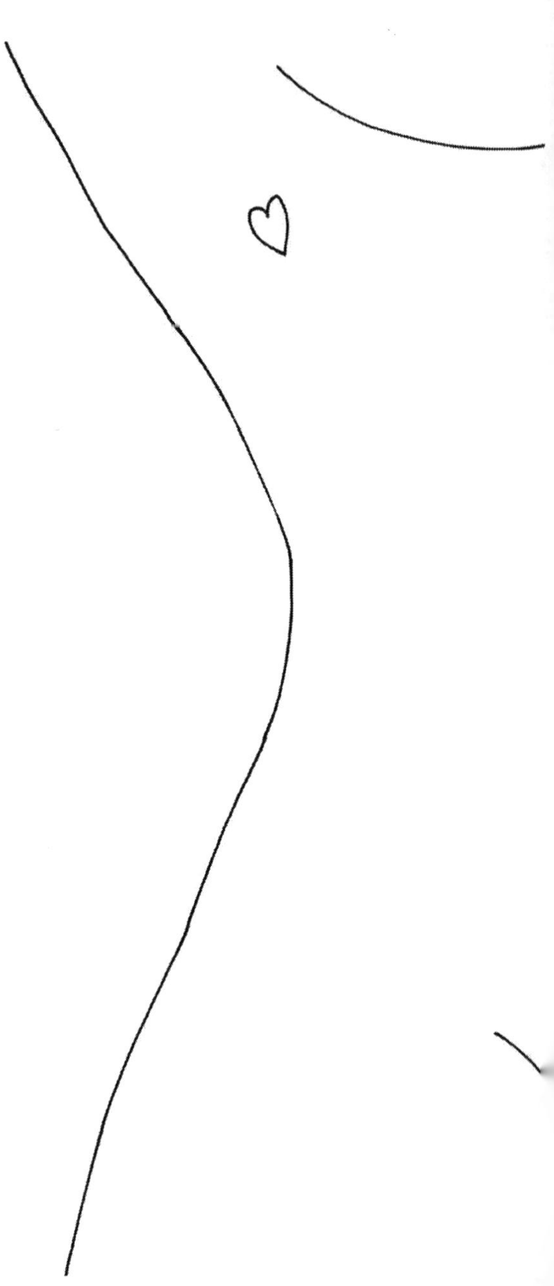

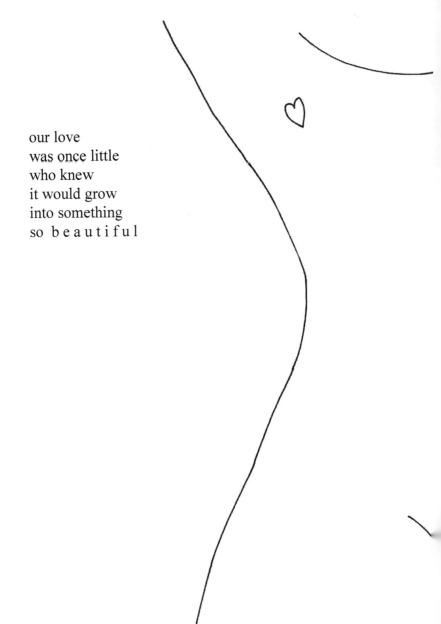

our love
was once little
who knew
it would grow
into something
so b e a u t i f u l

only if you knew
how beautiful your words sound
as they flow from your mouth
and into my ears

our dates turned into months
then years
but hopefully
it's a forever thing

if you found love
in the
oddest place
then
life brought you there
on purpose

it’s the distance that makes me miss you
it’s the distance that makes me think
what if
i don’t have you
in my life
anymore

as much as i
think about you
i wonder if
i’ll ever
manifest you
in my life

she was a flower
and he had patience
he knew if he watered her soul
she would grow and blossom

sometimes
i wonder
how often your mind wanders
to think about me

she sees me deep
she knows me well
i knew myself
now I see myself
as she sees me
i'm not lost
i'm not found
i'm enlightened

i am complete

your love must run deep
because you always give
and never seek

these lips have only felt yours
since the first day we kissed

my words could never define
the endless amount of love
i have for you

your body of water
crashes
slow
calm
and
deep

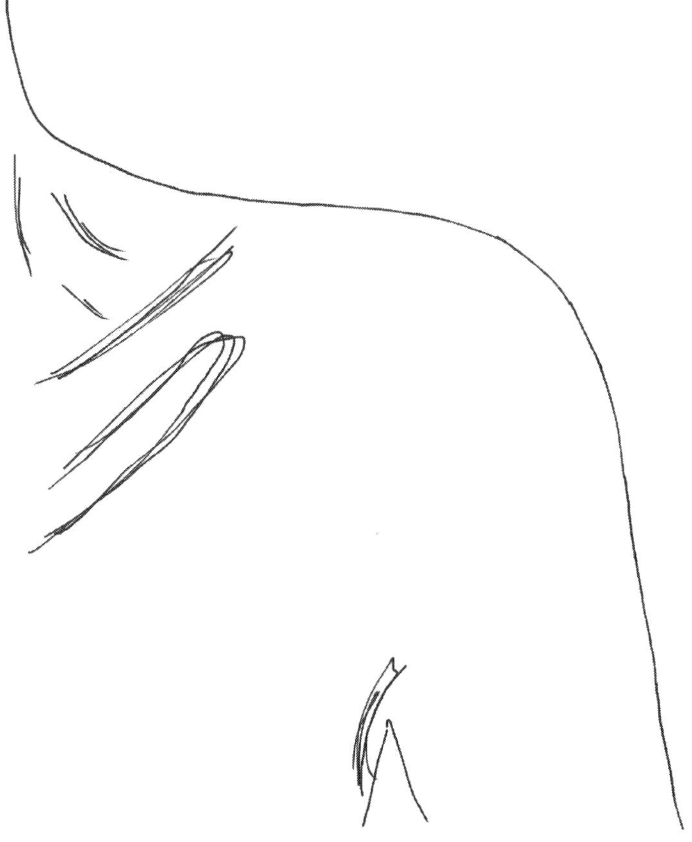

i never understood beauty
inside and out
until i met you

there's a secret place in my heart
where I keep our greatest memories
under lock and key

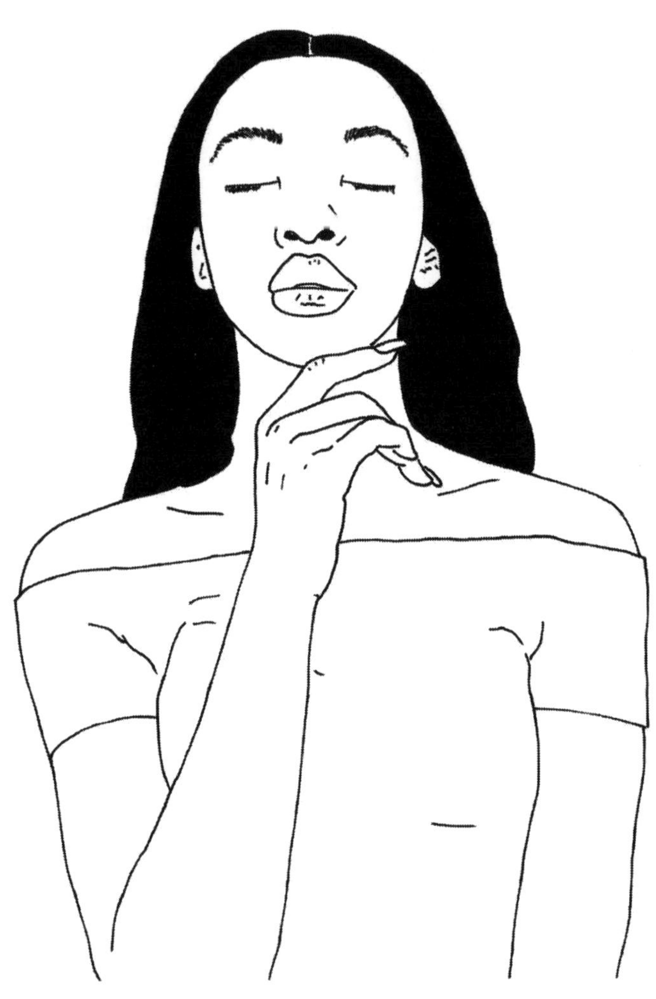

you can’t give someone all of you
when part of you
is still stuck in the past

her beauty on the inside
began to reflect on the outside
as if her soul had a mirror

I fell in love with
her words
her beauty
her strength
her wisdom
her touch
her smile
her kiss
her laugh
her humor
her love
her body
her affection
her glow

but most importantly her soul

i sense that we're meant to be
whenever i look into your eyes
i see a part of me that i've been seeking to find
the incompetence of my ability to love
leaves me with doubts but this time will be different
only if feelings were a part of a game
then we all would give it our all and never hold back
i guess that's why so called players win
and innocent people lose

she pulled me out my comfort zone
i've changed her in many ways
we've came accustomed to each other
so much
we think we don't need each other
we want each other
until one of us fades away
and realized there is no one
without the other

my heart beated fast when we met
slow when we hugged
skipped when we kissed
and became full when we made love

if you could see yourself through my eyes
you would fall in love with yourself all over again

we both know love can be psychotic
at least we'll be crazy together

to receive love
you must give love
to feel love
you must be love

the person who
broke your heart
will never be able to
put it back the same way
it used to be

reupholstered heart

they love you more when you're a mess
because it's harder to break someone
who has it together

for every time
your heart was broken
there was a piece left behind
waiting to be discovered

my ex got married i heard
congratulations!
i think i made the best decision
for the both of us

how many times
do you need to be treated like
somebody's step stool
before you understand
the last time
was the first time
of many more?

repeat

he was never a prince charming
that could rescue you from distress
he was only good at telling fairy tales
and selling happy endings

forgive to forget
nothing is worth more than your happiness
and having the strength to
move on

life will move on
so will my feelings
towards you

how could i ever regret us
when you were
the best lesson
learned

forgiveness is like giving back
the unwanted pain
to the giver and moving on

let the breakup
turn you into a rainbow
after the storm

i used to say too much out of anger
knowing the truth would hurt you

her heart broke into pieces
only she knew how to put back together

THANKU

there would be no us
without our exes

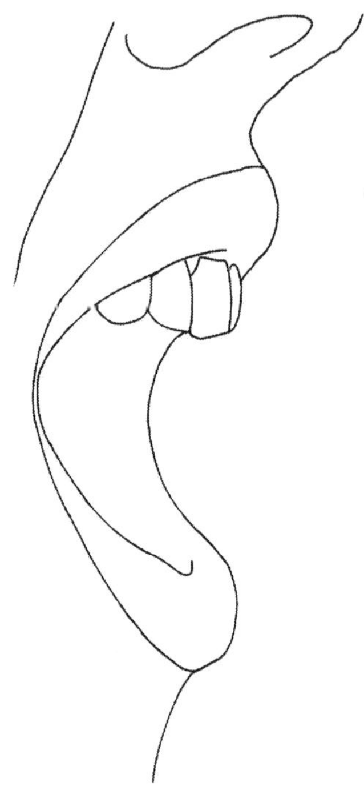

our love has been in chaos
hearts would scream if they could
they beat irregular
only to avoid beating in sync
we hate each other so much
it makes us love each other more
i could never see myself without you
but i need some time
without you

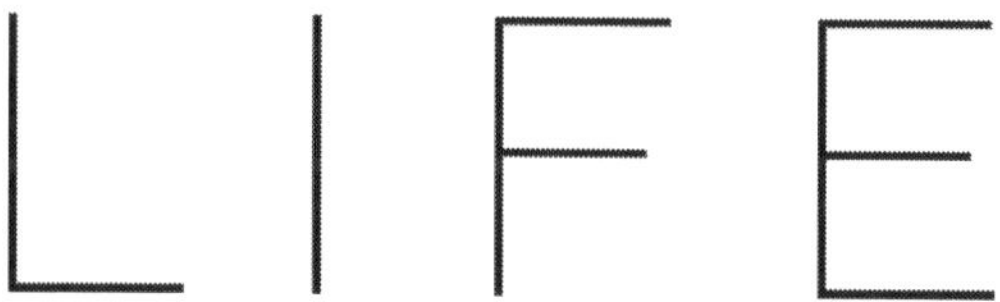

mind over matter is the only weapon i ever needed
my doubts were overturned by choices
my determination was powered by my decisions
my entire life changed in an instant

T H A N K U

my intuition
told me
so

being poor is only a mindset
not a lifestyle

whoever knows where hard work
and persistence will take them
it's about the journey
and not the end results

the journey along the way is meant to be
joyful, painful, emotional, and uncomfortable
what else will make success
feel like an accomplishment
in the end

not because i’m a quitter
but because the passion was lost
i made a logical decision
to invest my time
and effort
into things
that truly mattered to me
and things
i’m truly passionate about

when all things seem like they're

f
  a
l
  l
i
  n
g

they're really falling into place

some people hide
what others embrace

too many times
i sat still
wondering why
i did not do it sooner

never again

feel the fear
and overcome it
because one day
it will no longer exist

take off your fears
remove your ego
life feels good
when you're naked

the world feels like
it's closing in on you
when you're stagnate
keep moving
keep pushing

when life shows you ugly
it knows
you are not appreciating
the beauty

the dreamer lives a life that is full
only in the mind

look around
what you see
is how you view life
what they see
can be completely different
perspectives are based
off our own internal belief system

life is full of surprises
but only karma gives the gifts
stay on her good side

where there are no expectations
there are no disappointments

everything in life is an illusion
you see what you believe

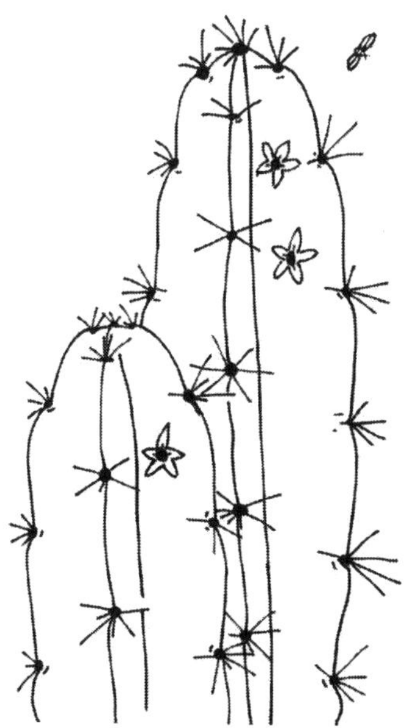

g r a t i t u d e
has always
been
a part
of my attitude
that's why
I'm blessed

i always pay it forward
so i don’t have to pay it in debt

cannot have good without evil
nor positivity without negativity

hate and negativity creates problems
love and positivity solve problems
you do the math

love has always been my heart's biggest idol
love is what it looks up to
and what it wants to be

my heart is the biggest impersonator
all it wants to be in life is love
the biggest lover i know

maybe i'm afraid to fall in love again
because my heart fell a little too hard last time

you're going through
what you're going through
right now
because there is
a lesson to be learned
and with every lesson learned
there is
a lesson taught

we all need to love each other
unconditionally and not intentionally

when we let our egos run freely
and let our hearts wander
jealousy is the point where they both intersect
for one could never be jealous of another
if the ego did not exist
and the heart was content

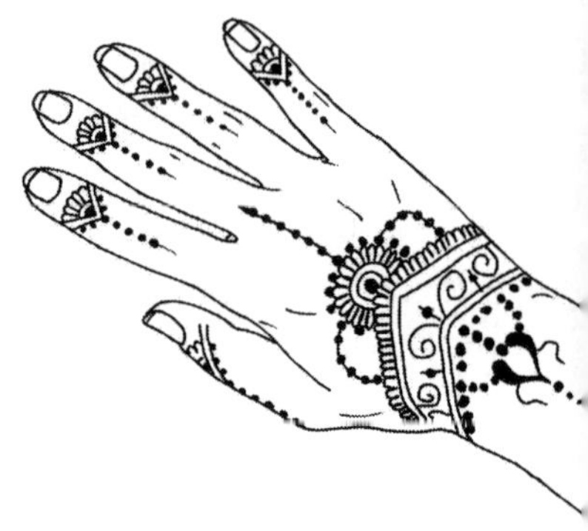

we all should love a little more each day
understand each other more when indifferent
take the time to appreciate
the little moments that are overlooked
and cherish this day
we all have been given

the moment you stop wanting it
is the moment you will have it
other words
the moment you start realizing you have it
is the moment you will

speak the truth at all time
and you shall see the truth
living a life of falsification
is like living a life with
bad karma

act out of universal love
and you will never be misguided
this world is a nurturer by nature
and always wants to give
the strongest thoughts
are driven into reality
intangible things
turn tangible
dreams that were once aspirations
turn into past tense
and we move forward to obtain the next one
the more blessings you seek
the more you will find
the lack of anything you speak
the less you will receive
it has always been this way
and will always be

pretending to be something you're not
will only hurt you in the end
once you attract
the fake
the unnecessary
the emptiness
the unwanted

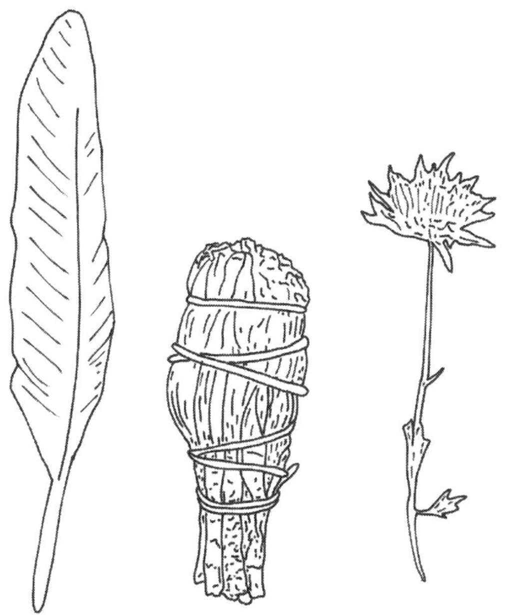

when you're attracting negative energy
just remember
you experience what you project

in this life
there is masculine energy
and female energy
i used to suppress my feminine energy
with the assumption if i didn't
it would make me less a man
now i know
embracing the balance between
the masculine and feminine energy
is not about sex
it's a balance of completeness
a yin and yang
a total eclipse of both energies
when not obscured
are both in alignment
and within us

one day i will pop
or float away
like a loose balloon in the sky

the lines that flow gracefully around her hips
are like lines on a map
that shows the roads her soul has traveled

THANKU

some
flowers

just
outgrow

others

some flowers die off
before they get a chance to blossom

she never knew she was a rose
until she blossomed

she watched the stars shine
before she believed in her own magic

angels sing
and i listen
because i know
the melody
holds the chords
to your heart

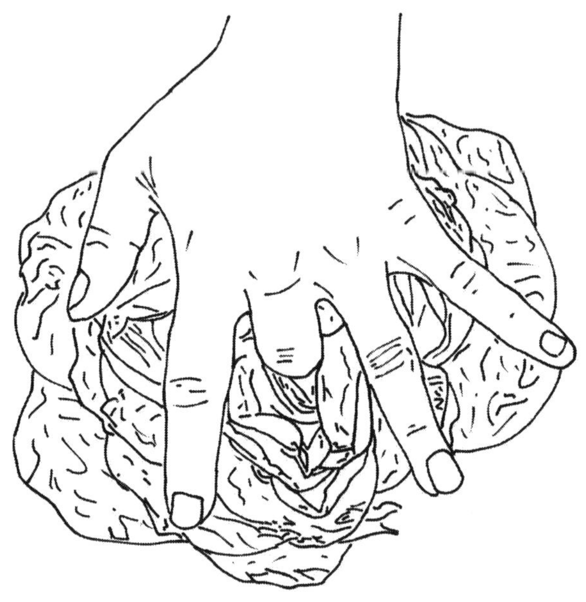

she said a little sex appeal
can make a good girl look bad
she's living proof

sometimes
all we need is
a reality check
to deposit

not all flowers are roses
but that doesn't make them less beautiful

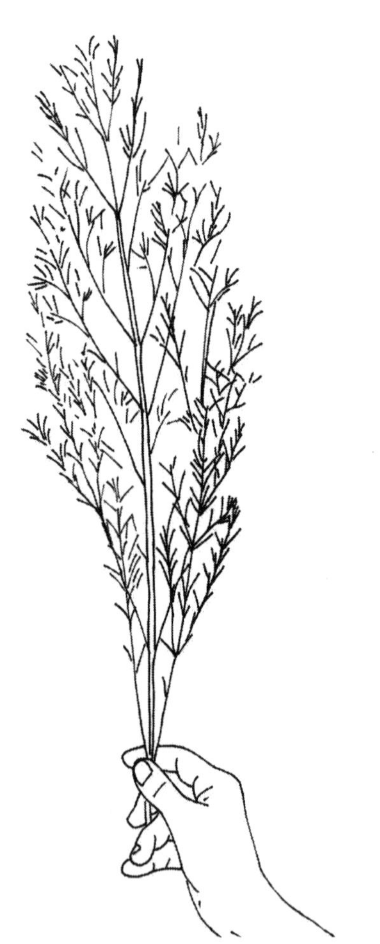

for every rain drop
that falls from the sky
i wish just one
would caress your cheek
and remind you
of me

she made a life full of regret
and now lives a life of forgiveness

she's a wildflower
whose beauty is
admirable
and untamable

you cannot be truly happy
when you have a past
you cannot accept

forgive and forget

have fun with life
and live with no regrets

never regret a life that is yours

better yourself to realize
you can do better

sometimes your past brings people
or situations to your present
so you can reflect
and appreciate how much you have changed

if i tell you my past
don't use it against me

she said my words were like magic
i never wanted to be a magician

give someone a seed
and it's up to them to plant it

when summer begins to fall
and knocks down all the leaves

it must be september

i shouldn't have to lose myself
to be with you
to eventually leave
to find the love i gave away

i feel lonelier
when i’m with you
and complete
when i’m without you

you sweared if i'd give you another chance

things would be different

rest in peace to my old self
because my new self just upgraded
while my old self died a slow death
And memories seem faded

memories only last
for as long as
they mean something
to you

not every girl half-naked
in a picture
is easy to get with
and not every man
in a picture
with money
is rich
or have
rich intentions

social media

people who intentionally try to hurt you
are already hurt themselves
and want someone to join their pain

don't become a bandage for their deep cuts

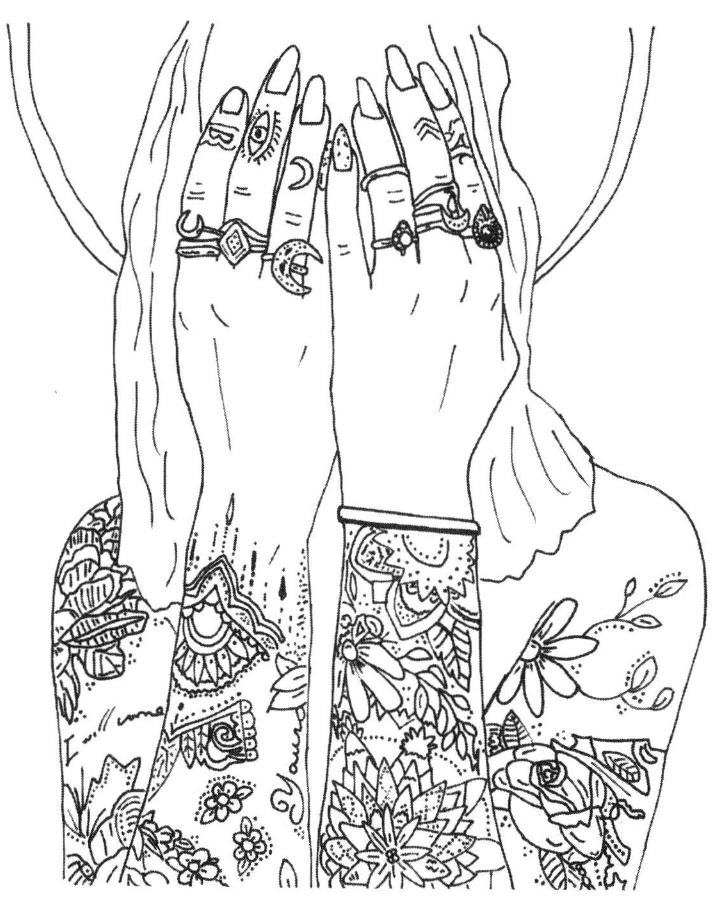

tears today
smiles tomorrow
amnesia next week
like none of this ever happened

everyday we create a past
to look back on

how are you
going to reflect
on this given moment
in time?

if you haven't learned something new today
or worked towards a goal
then your day is
most likely
going to a waste

learn something new

some want affection
but not commitment
that the downside of being independent
and not committed

i wonder where their dreams go to die
i never hear them speak of such

no one will ever tell you
both sides of the story

one-sided

through any transition
with much prayer, trust, and faith
you will make it out more powerful than before
life is about evolving
and not about revolving
around the same situations
the same experiences
the same people with no change
we are always protected
in our journey
in this existence
called life

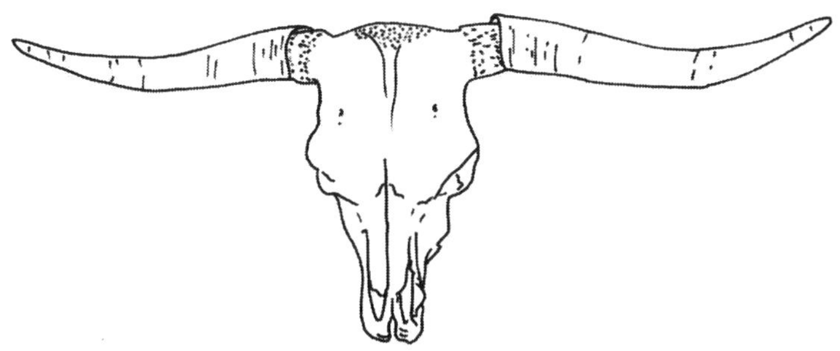

i pray that i forever
know of God's existence
in this lifetime
and thereafter

Made in the USA
Middletown, DE
03 December 2017